TED 1

Hi, my name is Tractor Ted. Let's see some massive machines at work.

TED 1

Look at this huge tractor.

It has so many wheels.

This tractor has huge wheels too.

What is this tractor doing?

TED 1

It has massive cultivators on the back.

Look at this tractor. It can only just fit around the corner.

TED 1

It has caterpillar tracks as well.

Here it is working in the field.

TED 1

These tractors are pulling huge potato planters.

They can get the job done quickly.

What is this machine?

It is a sprayer.

It has very long arms.

It is a seed drill.

Here is a muck spreader.

It has a very large tank.

The muck goes into the ground.

Look at this muck spreader.

It has only one wheel at the front.

The muck is spread
onto the fields.

TED 1

Here is another tractor with caterpillar tracks.

It has some on the front and some on the back.

TED 1

Even the trailer has caterpillar tracks.

Look how massive it is!

GAMES TO PLAY

Which is the odd one out?

TED 1

Can you remember the jobs these machines are doing?